Baby and Me

Planning support groups for new parents and their babies

by
Dr Hannah Mortimer

Q/Ed

A QEd Publication

Published in 2005

ISBN 1 898873 46 1

British Library Cataloguing
A catalogue record for this book is available from the British Library.

Q√
Ed

Published by QEd Publications, 39 Weeping Cross, Stafford ST17 0DG
Tel: 01785 620364
Website: www.qed.uk.com
Email: orders@qed.uk.com

Printed in the United Kingdom by Stowes (Stoke-on-Trent).

Contents

Introduction

The aim of the series

This series is for those working in Sure Start centres and other early years services who want to work with parents or carers of young children in groups. In recent years, there has been a blossoming of Sure Start schemes all over the country with massive recruitment and intensive staff training as more and more schemes come on line. These books have been put together by practitioners who already have parent and carer groups up and running. They are the result of trying out approaches and evaluating their success and the hope is that they will provide practical ideas for colleagues starting new groups to prevent them having to reinvent the wheel. Inevitably, you will each be serving very individual communities with particular sets of needs, but it is hoped that you will find plenty of ideas in this series that will get you started.

Baby and Me groups have proved to be an excellent way of introducing group work in a community. They are an enjoyable and non-threatening method of 'getting families through the door', enabling you to move on to more supportive ways of working later on. They also serve as a gentle introduction to running a group and building up your own confidence in group working. The benefits of working in groups with parents or carers of babies are to promote friendship and mutual support; reduce isolation; help parents in supporting their babies; and share information and advice in a palatable and non-threatening manner.

Since the daily work of many Sure Start schemes is centred around family support and since this so often occurs in groups or 'drop-ins' held at a Sure Start base or community centre, these books are about how you make that delicate move from the informal 'drop-in' to the kind of structure that will enable you to improve confidences, relationships and quality of communications between parents or carers and their children under five.

The series includes books on:

RUMPUS Groups behaviour management groups for parents or carers and their young children.

Step by Step Groups groups that provide ideas and support to parents or carers to enable them to encourage their child's development (if the child is vulnerable or might have special educational needs [SEN]).

Music and Play Groups groups that provide circle time and structured play activities that improve relationships between parents or carers and their children.

Baby and Me parent groups that promote early development, relationships and communication in their babies.

Making Connections therapeutic groups for parents or carers to help them form stronger attachments with their children.

Sure Start

In Sure Start schemes, families are targeted to receive information, support and guidance to help them make the most of their young child's developmental, learning and social potential, and also to improve upon their parenting and child-rearing skills. The aim is to improve the life chances of young children in areas of 'risk' through improving their access to education, health services, family support and advice on nurturing. Typical Sure Start schemes provide a range of services and provision – there might be outreach and home visiting; support to families; opportunities for quality play, learning and childcare experiences for young children; advice on child and family health; and support for families who have a young child with SEN or other disability.

What is a Baby and Me group?

These groups were based on the need for post-natal support, what we know about promoting attachments in the early months and the *Music Makers* approach (see page 40).

Here is how one group of practitioners described their Baby and Me group:

We meet each week to offer new parents of babies information, friendship and support. We address health issues as required, taking our lead from parents and covering this at a more personal level than we might have done when we ran post-natal clinics. Topics include childhood illnesses, immunisations, resuscitation, speech and language development, baby massage, diet and juicing, nursery rhymes and lap songs, breastfeeding support. We use music as a way of strengthening connections and sharing pleasure. The group is small, informal and intimate and we try to encourage it to be parent-led. Friendships have developed between the parents – usually we only have mums though all parents are welcome.

How to use this book

You now have an overview of what a Baby and Me group might look like. Here is an outline of what to expect in the book:

- In the first chapter, you will consider when and why you might like to run such a group and how it might fit into the Sure Start framework of provision, or indeed into the early years service that you offer.

- Chapter 2 helps you plan ahead – what you need in terms of equipment, personnel, premises and skills.

- In Chapter 3 there are suggestions for the music session at the beginning of the group which are accessible at any level of musical ability – you do not need to be musical yourself.

- In Chapter 4 there are suggestions for baby massage which some groups weave into their Baby and Me session and others run as separate sessions altogether.

- Chapter 5 has ideas for other topics you might include.

- Chapter 6 contains suggestions for evaluation and reporting back to management committees.

- Finally, there are some helpful resources and contacts listed at the back.

Throughout the book there are ideas and suggestions from practitioners who have actually developed and run these groups. These should help you to understand why certain approaches were used and what the particular challenges and opportunities were in running the groups.

You will find a certain amount of overlap in the texts of the five books in this series. The repetition is intentional and should help the reader feel confident in 'mixing and matching' approaches.

Chapter 1

Why have a Baby and Me group?

In the first chapter we cover *when* and *why* you might like to run such a group and how it might fit into the Sure Start framework of provision, or indeed into the more general early years service that you offer.

> *Baby and Me was developed to offer support, friendship and information for parents with new babies.*
>
> (Sure Start practitioner)

Now that we know more about patterns of attachment between parents and their children, we can begin to identify those who are successfully 'connected' or 'bonded' from those who are not. One manager and health visitor, Karen Bibbings, has devised this simple activity to explain what 'connection' looks like.

The Glums

Below is a scenario that could be used as a staff discussion point.

Imagine you are sitting in a restaurant. In one corner, there is a couple who are obviously deeply in love. We will call them 'the Lovers'. How do you know that they are in love? What behaviours do you actually observe? Make a list of these on a large sheet of paper.

Now imagine you are in the same restaurant and in another corner is a couple who are clearly not getting on very well. We will call them 'the Glums'. What do you actually see or hear this time? Make another list.

Things to consider:
- Think about parents or carers and children who are 'attached' or 'connected' to each other. Do you observe similar behaviours as 'the Lovers' and 'the Glums'?

- You now know what a connected child and carer look like. Can you also recognise when such a connection is not there?

- Think of ways you can support attachments/connections by helping parents or carers 'tune in' to their children and share pleasure in each other.

From an activity by Karen Bibbings, Health Visitor,
Stockton-on-Tees Sure Start (with permission)

Patterns of attachment

'Attachment Theory' argues that children develop a style of relating to important attachment figures in their lives, which secures for them the best parenting available under the circumstances. The study of attachments has opened up a whole new way of assessing family relationships and providing therapeutic support. The patterns of attachment remain remarkably consistent over time until the child is about six, and so can be observed, identified and worked with.

Where attachment is working securely, an infant's cries and demands will be met reliably with sensitivity and warmth by the carer, and the growing child develops in confidence and independence. If a parent is unresponsive or rejecting of their cries of distress, that child may act as if they are independent long before they are emotionally ready to be. They may pay little attention when their parent leaves them at nursery and seldom look at their parent or try to involve them in their play. This is known as a pattern of 'anxious-avoidant' attachment.

If a parent is inconsistent in their responses, perhaps because of periods of depression or frequent absences, the child learns to cry or shout louder with their demands, producing a pattern of 'ambivalent' attachment. There is also a pattern of 'disorganised' or 'controlling' attachment in which children develop a very controlling style over their parent in order to maintain some degree of predictability or structure in their lives. This pattern is common with parents who might have suffered loss, trauma or abuse themselves, or lack a 'secure base' of their own from which to provide nurture and care to others in their lives. Understanding about attachments does not mean that we should go forth and proclaim that a parent or child 'has an attachment disorder'. However, it does help us to understand that there is an emotional component to the behaviour or the relationship which may involve us trying to intervene on an emotional level as well as a behavioural or teaching level.

Which families benefit most from Baby and Me?

We have found Baby and Me groups are most effective for:

- parents and carers of babies who would like to meet up regularly with similar families;

- families who appreciate occasional and ongoing information from a health visitor or other Sure Start professional;

We have not found Baby and Me groups helpful for:

- mothers with severe post-natal depression (an alternative service would be offered such as a 'Sunshine' group or individual therapeutic work);

- families who are told to attend rather than who choose to.

We found that it fitted most easily where there was a whole scaffold of support – for example, antenatal care groups, services and groups to support those with post-natal depression, RUMPUS (for toddler behaviour difficulties), Music and Play and Making Connections (for more entrenched attachment difficulties). You will find that there is further information on some of these groups in other books in this series.

Baby and Me in Sure Start

The Baby and Me model developed naturally to fit the SureStart framework in Stockton-on-Tees Borough Council where there are many schemes serving urban and diverse communities. We saw it as fitting into a wider framework of provision in which parents and carers fell into three main categories:

- Hard to reach – they need support but may not ask for it or even want it.

- Mainstream – they both need and want support.

- Easy to reach – they probably do not really need support but want it anyway.

This kind of thinking enables one to draw up a grid of support, making sure that each category of parent has access to support at different family life stages. For example, with the 'hard-to-reach' families, you might opt for a home visiting model as a first stage towards involving that family in more group-based activity and support. We saw Baby and Me as fitting into the framework for supporting 'mainstream' and 'easy-to-reach' families at the 'new arrivals' stage.

A grid of support: what your spread of provision might include

Life stage	Hard-to-reach families	Mainstream families	Easy-to-reach families
Pregnancy	• Home visiting	• Bump club (antenatal support)	• Bump club
New arrivals	• Home visiting • Sunshine group (for post-natal depression support)	• Baby and Me	• Baby and Me
Toddlers and pre-school	• Home visiting • Making Connections group*	• Music and Play* • RUMPUS* (for behavioural support) • Step by Step* (for developmental teaching)	• Music and Play*

* There are books covering these type of groups in this series.

In other words, Baby and Me sessions are helpful for parents and carers who want to join in and who may or may not need low-level support from their health visitor or Sure Start worker. They serve as a gateway into Sure Start services and are a practical way of 'bringing families on board' in order to develop further Sure Start services for them.

Chapter 2

Planning ahead

Chapter 2 helps you plan ahead – what you need in terms of equipment, personnel, premises and skills. Suppose you have a cohort of several families for whom you would like to plan a Baby and Me group. This is what you need to do next.

Finding a room

We have found that the best space to use is a fairly intimate, carpeted room with a warm temperature and atmosphere. Baby changing facilities are included in the room and the physical and emotional atmosphere feels welcoming for breastfeeding.

Staffing

The group is health visitor-led with support from either childcare facilitators, parent liaison workers or other Sure Start employees. We aim for one professional for two to three families.

Booking equipment

Collect a selection of safe baby toys for swiping (baby gyms and activity centres), shaking (rattles and bells), looking at (baby mirrors, colourful toys) and handling (fabrics, play mats, soft toys). We used the local toy library. We also purchased brightly coloured chiffon scarves to support our music and play activities. Be aware that babies might swallow small, loose items and that sucked equipment needs to be cleaned and disinfected regularly and certainly between each session.

Transport

Look for a base that is easy to get to using public transport and which has safe and convenient parking for family cars and buggies. You might also be able to make use of local hospital transport services or Sure Start transport vehicles. If the cost of transport is going to be prohibitive for some families, consider building a travel allowance for families into the budget.

Creche facilities

Where possible, a creche is helpful for older siblings not yet in school. This gives the parent or carer special time with the baby and time to be nurtured and supported away from some of the pressures of parenting.

Refreshments

There is an element of nurturing within the Baby and Me group and, to do this, you need a convenient kitchen nearby with facilities for making parents drinks and refreshments. Be aware of safety rules about hot drinks close to babies. You might cover the cost of refreshments using a voluntary donation of a suggested amount. We felt that this helped parents feel that they were able to contribute something themselves and we then subsidised any shortfall.

Inviting the families

You need to think about what information you are going to tell the families ahead of the group.

We had some difficulties using the word 'advice'. It sounded too medical – as if we were professionals telling parents what they should be doing. We wanted it to be more parent-led and we wanted to respond to what they needed. So we went for the word 'information' instead – we are providing a service and they are the client, as it were.

(Sure Start professional)

Here is an example of the kind of information sheet you might use (with acknowledgements to SureStart Stockton-on-Tees). If you wish, you can adapt it and use your own logo to make an introductory pamphlet. Where necessary or desirable, you should take the trouble of producing the pamphlet in different languages. You might find it best to carry out a home visit in order to meet the family and pass on written information.

You are invited to

BABY and ME

Who can come: Parents and babies

What's it all about? Quality time for you and your baby!

When? _____

Where? _____

Creche available for older brothers and sisters not yet at school.

Feel supported

It's too easy to stay at home feeling isolated, especially with a new baby. Why not come along and have a chat in a relaxed environment?

Meet new friends

This can feel impossible when you are half asleep . . . wondering what day it is!

Join us and we will remind you . . . and give you all the attention and care you need . . . so you can do the same for your baby.

Not to mention the latest news.

Share the latest tricks of parenthood

Our past discussions have covered:
- baby massage
- baby resuscitation
- immunisations
- nursery rhymes

For more information contact:

Chapter 3

Musical beginnings

This chapter gives you many suggestions for the music session. The main aim of the music part of your session is to encourage parents or carers to interact with their babies through musical activity. This can be difficult when you lack confidence, if you feel shy or if you do not have much of a repertoire in the way of songs. That is why your whole environment needs to be intimate, informal, reassuring and relaxing. Babies have started their gestational lives surrounded by maternal sounds – the rhythmic beating of the heart and rushing of the blood. They will, therefore, respond well to the sounds of their parents' voices after birth, especially if they can feel confident in singing to their baby.

Why music?

Over the years, the author has found that professionals are horrified at the suggestion that they should have a music time as part of their session: 'We're not musical!' 'The families will be embarrassed!' 'The children won't respond.' Time and time again, she has persuaded groups to 'have a go' and time and time again they have reported back that the music *makes all the difference*.

Music is an amazing thing – it stills a crying baby. It captures a toddler's attention. It holds the interest of children who, in any other situation, might be experiencing considerable behaviour or communication difficulties. It provides opportunities for even very young children to join together sociably in a group, long before they are old enough to attend an early years setting. Music encourages children who do not like to look and to listen to do just that. It provides a 'level playing field' for professionals and families to 'break the ice' together – after all, neither is the 'expert' and both will find themselves sharing a laugh or a grimace as the process does not go as expected! But staggeringly, even babies are captivated and, sometimes for the first time ever, parents and carers are seeing them look, listen and concentrate in a way they have never done before. This gives the parents a sense of pride and something to build on at home. It also allows parents to share pleasure with their babies, one of the most productive ways of building up attachments and 'connections'.

What you need

Start collecting very simple musical instruments or noise-making toys until you have a range of safe and attractive percussive and shaking instruments suitable for under-twos. Babies respond well to chewable instruments that can be mouthed and felt as well as shaken, dropped and found again. They need to be small enough to handle or solid enough to be swiped at or knocked. Take care that there are no loose parts that might be swallowed. Bells can be attached to limbs to make jingling sounds as the baby moves. We choose instruments that suit the child's stage and what they are happy to accept. You will also need some musical accompaniment. Perhaps you can harness some local musical talent and encourage a fellow professional or parent to play a gentle guitar or keyboard. If not, a cassette recorder or CD-player works well. Make sure the quality of sound is good and have one adult on standby to manage the machine so that the music leader does not need to worry about it. We made our own CD with basic nursery rhymes and action songs and we all sang along to it. We did not simply let it run in the same old order, but used it to back up the songs we had planned for that session. Aim to keep the music as live and individual as possible.

The right space

You will also need a suitable area of your room to hold the music session in. Use a circle of baby mats to signal to the families where to lie their babies. Arrange these on a carpet so that parents or carers can sit or kneel on the floor, looking over their babies. Everyone in the room should join the music session – the only exceptions are babies asleep in buggies.

How to organise the music session

One of you should be the music leader – depending on who is confident enough to have a go. You might find it helpful to have a large puppet, teddy or doll to model the movements and the interactions that a parent might like to do with or to the baby. Use the session planning sheet below to help you plan the activities, aiming for 15 to 20 minutes' duration.

Music Time
Date: _____
Warm-up
Hello song
Action rhymes/songs
Looking or listening games
Music for being bounced to
Band time

Write in what you will do in each section and who will do it. This allows the whole session to flow smoothly.

Warm-up

First choose a well-known favourite to signal the beginning of a session and become your 'theme tune'. *If you're happy and you know it* involves actions and familiar words, is easy to pick up and seems to be known by most of the families. This should be your warm-up song at the beginning of every session. The warm-up song both lets the babies know that music is about to begin and the familiarity helps them feel secure.

Hello song

You then need a greeting song to include and welcome all your families into music time. Make sure to include the names of any visiting siblings, toddlers or babies, even if they are sleeping. You should greet each baby with a name, a look and a smile, perhaps a wave and a toe wiggle too (unless they are sleeping). Ideally, you should encourage the babies to look at you as you sing to them by moving your head until you are in the baby's focus of attention. You should also encourage the adults to join in the singing of this greeting song. Here is a simple version of a 'hello song', sung to the tune of *Tommy Thumb*.

> *Hello Jack, Hello Jack,* (move in and establish eye contact)
> *Where are you?*
> *Here I am, here I am!* (wave)
> *How do you do!* (take a hand or wiggle a toe)

The next song allows you to tune in to the mood of each baby in the group and not make any demands on the parents either. It is sung to the tune of *One finger, one thumb, keep moving* or can be fitted to the tune of *The farmer's in his dell*. Choose an action that reflects what the baby is doing.

> *Let's bounce/rock/wave/clap . . . hello to Carly*
> *Let's bounce/rock/wave/clap . . . hello to Carly*
> *Let's bounce/rock/wave/clap . . . hello to Carly*
> *And welcome her today.*

Action rhymes/songs

Next move on to a few action songs or nursery rhymes. Keep the actions simple, starting with only one or two verses and building up until the adults are familiar with the songs. Always try to have one well-known action rhyme and only introduce one new one per session. Encourage all the adults to model the actions and insist (with shared humour) that any fellow professionals join in fully. Take the songs slowly to give everyone time to respond. Here are some ideas.

> *Cobbler cobbler mend my shoe* (with a toe wiggle)
> *This little piggie* (touching toes in turn)
> *Roly poly* (rolling the baby from side to side)
> > *Roly poly this way*
> > *Roly poly back*
> > *Roly poly, ever so slowly*
> > *Roly poly back!*
> *Round and round the garden* (tracing on their hands)
> *Incy wincy spider* (creeping fingers up their arms)
> *Put a finger on your nose, on your nose* (gently touching the body parts named)
> *Heads, shoulders, knees and toes* (touching the babies as you sing)

Some action rhymes adapt beautifully to a lying position and others can be done with the baby sitting or lying in a lap.

Listening games

If babies are to learn to make sense of their worlds, they will first need to develop their looking and listening skills. Here are some simple ideas of games that will promote these to start you off.

- *Tambourine shake* – shake a tambourine and encourage everyone to shake all over and gently bounce their babies until you bang it to stop.

- *Where's the sound?* – ask certain parents or colleagues to shake or bang an instrument at one end of the circle and encourage the babies to look in that direction.

- *Dinner on the train* – start with soft, slow voices and build up to loud, fast voices as you chant this rhyme and move the babies on your knees:

  Coffee (4 times)
  Cheese and biscuits (4 times)
  Chocolate pudding (4 times)
  Fish and chips (4 times)
  SOUUUUUUUP! (once with one hand held high as you 'blow the whistle')

Looking games

We purchased a set of brightly coloured chiffon scarves which we wash (gently in soapy water and rinse well) after each session. These can be handled, drawn gently across faces for 'peep bo' games and waved in the air for colourful effects. Babies (and carers) of all ages love them.

Make up your tune to this rhyme as you encourage the mothers to draw a scarf lightly over the baby's face and then draw it away.

> *Where's Jacob gone?*
> *Where's Jacob gone?*
> *Where's Jacob gone? ... (pause)*
> *Jacob says ... BOO!*

Try moving around the outside of the circle singing or shaking a jingly instrument. Celebrate as the older babies turn their heads to watch you. Introduce new sounds and sights to catch the babies' interest but be careful not to startle them. Do not worry too much about the babies that are sleeping – it is staggering what young babies can sleep through!

Music for being bounced to

Any bouncy nursery rhyme or song will do. Bounce the babies gently on a knee or over a shoulder as you sing together. Babies love gentle movement and anticipation. Older babies can begin to anticipate a surprise movement and use their vocalisations, eye contact or movements to indicate that they would like the action repeated. Encourage the mothers to pause between rhymes to ask 'more?' Here is a regular and traditional favourite for babies old enough to sit on a lap with support. Ask mothers to sit their babies across their legs facing them, either cradling them safely in their outstretched arms or holding their hands if they are older. It is usually chanted rather than sung.

> *This is the way the ladies ride, nim, nim, nim* (gently jogging the babies up and down at a walking pace)
> *This is the way the gentlemen ride, trot, trot, trot* (jogging them up slightly faster and higher)
> *This is the way the huntsmen ride, gallopy, gallopy, gallopy* (with a faster movement and sharing the laughter)
> *And THIS is the way the farmer rides, giddyup, giddyup, giddyup, giddyup*
> *And . . . DOWN into the ditch!* (cradling the baby's head and holding safely as you let them fall down towards the floor, holding eye contact as you do so)

If you have political sensitivities, you can amend these words to suit a more modern version (as is the case with so many traditional rhymes). We tried a version along the lines of: *This is the way the buses drive*; *This is the way the ambulances drive* etc.

Band time
For babies who are sitting up and holding things, offer rattles and chewable instruments to explore as you sing a range of nursery rhymes. From time to time, gently hold hand-over-hand to demonstrate how to make a sound with the instrument.

Start the tape or CD. Encourage the adults to play when the music plays and stop when it stops. Watch out for any babies looking and listening and point out how clever they are. Once the group has settled in, stand up and march round the room together (all of you) holding or shaking your instruments as you go and bouncing the babies gently as you cradle or hold them. Older babies are fascinated by this and any older toddlers can join in independently and confidently.

Calming down time

Move into some more calming songs before you finish, such as gentle rocking songs and lullabies. You can also have a few of these up your sleeve in case you need to switch into them earlier for unsettled babies. Babies need to share quiet moments with their parents or carers as well as lively ones. You can 'pitch' your choice of action rhyme or song with the general mood of the group, making sure not to overstimulate the babies with too much sudden noise. Here are some ideas for quieter moments when you can rock gently:

Lavender's blue
Rock a bye baby
Twinkle twinkle little star
Row row row your boat

This last song has been adapted in our groups to include a wider range of feelings and moods:

Row row row your boat, gently down the stream
Merrily merrily merrily merrily, life is but a dream

Row row row your boat, gently down the stream
If you see a crocodile, don't forget to scream (muffled squeal)

Row row row your boat, gently down the stream
If you see a big giraffe, don't forget to laugh (laughter and giggles)

Row row row your boat, gently down the stream
If you see a hippopotamus, don't forget to make a lot of fuss!
(pretend to cry)
(Finish with first verse again.)

Goodbye song

Sing goodbye to everyone in the group. You can adapt another song such as *Twinkle twinkle* and sing:

Now it's time to say goodbye
Sanjit and Mum, off you fly

Here is an alternative version, sung to the tune of *Goodnight ladies*:

Goodbye Jamie, goodbye Mum,
Goodbye Jamie, it's time to say goodbye.
Merrily we roll along, roll along, roll along,
Merrily we roll along, all the way back home.

Again, try to encourage eye contact briefly as you sing each baby's name, unless they are snoozing or suckling.

Tips for music leaders

The success of the music session depends less on whether you can sing and more on how well you can 'hold the floor' with confidence and inspire confidence in others. Holding everyone's attention, keeping a balance and maintaining a flow are all important. However shy you feel inside, calmly establish eye contact with as many as possible in the circle showing that you are including them with you rather than singing at them. Everyone would quickly lose interest if you sat and sang songs solidly to a tape. By varying the presentation from quick to slow, song to chant, quiet song to loud song, you can keep a flow going. You will find you can hold attention for ten minutes or so when you first get going, gradually building up to around 15 minutes or even 20. Do not attempt longer at this age and stage. There are ideas for resources to help your music making on page 41.

Chapter 4

Baby massage

Baby massage is proving a wonderful method of increasing pleasurable physical contact between parent and baby and for building and strengthening attachments. Some Baby and Me groups have incorporated a baby massage into each session, once they have a member of staff or parent volunteers properly trained. Other parents and staff have opted for separate sessions in a warm and comfortable room where everyone can feel relaxed and more intimate. *It is important that the leader is properly trained.* More and more health visitors are receiving this training and some services are arranging joint training with both professionals and parent volunteers in the hope of rolling out baby massage into more community and home groups. Do not attempt to deliver this without the full training so that you are fully aware of all the safety aspects. This is an introduction to what baby massage 'looks' and 'feels' like in practice.

A gentle touch

When teaching parents and carers to massage their babies, it is important to help them to develop the right touch and movement. It is best to make stroking movements with fingers and thumbs – this is called effleurage. Massage is best done on a safe, soft surface and in the group we used baby changing mats covered with soft towels and laid on the carpet in a circle with babies on the inside and carers on the outside. The leader uses a life-size doll to model the touches and can be easily seen and heard by all the adults in the circle. At home, parents and carers might like to choose a special time to do it regularly – say two or three times a week at bathtime or bedtime. Massage should never be forced onto a baby and should be stopped if the mood does not feel right. Massage should be done in a warm, quiet place when there is no need to rush. You might wish to run a massage session every month or two in order to introduce any new parents or carers to the approach.

Safety first

Make the point that a baby should never be left unattended if you are massaging on a bed or table top. You should not massage if the baby is unwell since massage might spread the infection. It is also unwise to massage if the baby has fed within the previous hour. Babies with temperatures (for example, if they are unwell, teething or it is very hot) should not be massaged; neither should a baby with a skin infection. On the other hand, gentle massage is excellent for relieving colic, for soothing an unsettled baby, for helping constipation and for boosting health, well-being and the immune system. A light vegetable oil such as rape seed or sunflower oil is best. You should not use aromatherapy oils unless you have the advice of a qualified aromatherapist or reflexologist since some oils are too strong for babies. Baby oil is too greasy and does not absorb well.

Learn your script

The leader should be familiar with the script so that she or he can talk the carers through their massage, modelling the approach with the doll. All this will have been learned as part of the baby massage training. Before you begin, make sure that the room is welcoming and warm. Have a soft towel for each baby to lie on and to be swaddled in afterwards. Place a small plastic cup with a couple of tablespoons of oil beside each mat. You might find it helpful to play relaxing music in the background as you talk. Here is the kind of script we use.

Gently undress your baby down to the nappy. Lie your babies on their backs and kneel down at their feet so that they can see your face. If your baby prefers to lie with face towards you, that is fine too. Wrap the towel around them to make them feel cosy. Take a little of the oil and rub it between your hands until it feels warm. Start with the left leg – gently unwrap it and hold the foot in your hand for a second. This lets your baby know what is going to happen next. If they kick and move, try to go with their movements and do not restrain them. Lift the leg slightly and stroke from buttock to ankle two or three times. Now use a gentle pinching or plucking movement along the length of the baby's thigh and calf just for one leg length. Hold each toe in turn and gently draw your fingers off as if pulling each toe in turn. Massage gently the ball of the foot – the soft part behind the toes helps to stimulate the immune system and the heel area stimulates the bowel. Talk softly to your babies all the time, smiling, returning their sounds and looking at each other. Finally, sandwich the foot between your hands for a second or two to signal that you have finished that leg. Move onto the other leg and repeat the same script.

Now use a similar script to cover the massage of each arm in turn. Hold one arm up slightly for a second and then stroke down from the shoulder to the wrist two or three times. Gently pinch up and down the arm for one full arm length. Stroke the arms again and then stroke the back of the hand. Use your thumb to gently massage the palm of the baby's hand. Gently 'pinch off' each finger in turn and finish by holding the hand between both of yours to signal the end of that limb. Repeat for the other arm.

At this stage, carers might wish to remove or loosen the nappy so that they can begin the body massage. Add more oil to your hands. Gently smooth up the baby's body, outwards at the shoulders and down the outsides of the arms. Repeat a few times. Do not touch the baby's neck. Next place your hands each side and across baby's tummy, fingers meeting in the middle. Glide your hands from side to side and back again in a criss-cross manner. Now stroke clockwise around the tummy button area, gradually spiralling outwards. This is the direction that the food travels through the bowel – never massage in an anti-clockwise direction. Finish off with another full stroking movement as before and then hold both hands onto the tummy for a while to signal the end of this episode.

If your baby is happy to go onto the tummy, then turn him or her over. It is OK to place your baby on the tummy if you are there watching, though some do not like it. Using both hands, stroke up the back from buttocks to shoulders and out over the arms three or four times. With your thumbs each side of the backbone, caterpillar walk up the spine – with a light touch each side of the backbone but never pressing onto the bone itself. This movement is like playing the piano with your knuckles. Again, do a gliding criss-cross movement with both hands across and up the whole back. Gently knead each buttock and then finish by stroking up the back to the shoulders as before and holding your hands gently on their back before finishing.

Wrap the babies up warm and place them on their backs again. Stroke your baby's head from the centre of the forehead to the temples with your thumb or finger three or four times. Circle gently around the face with the fingertips, along the eyebrows and gently back under the eyes. Repeat several times, taking care not to get oil too near to the eyes by making sure you have only a little on your fingers – probably just what is already on your hands. Try a gentle circle around each earlobe. Finish by gently cupping your baby's ears with your hands to signal the end.

You will find that the whole process takes 15 to 20 minutes. Try to find a special time to enjoy this together two or three times a week. If your baby is unsettled, simply stop. You might also try a shorter massage such as just the feet for that day. Remember that massage is not just for babies – try a head massage or a foot massage on a fretful older child or a stressed teenager.

Chapter 5

Activities

Baby and Me groups offer new parents information, friendship and support. The ethos is to take the lead from parents and therefore to arrange topics or information around subjects of interest and need to them. Inevitably this will involve the range of topics traditionally covered in post-natal support groups such as day-to-day baby care, adjusting to life with the new baby, childhood illnesses, immunisations, resuscitation, diet and juicing, and breastfeeding support. We use music as a way of strengthening connections and sharing pleasure (many ideas for this have been covered in Chapter 3). Some groups are now also incorporating baby massage and this, too, has been covered in the previous chapter. In this chapter, we cover some of the other, less familiar topics that parents might like to include in your sessions:

- 'Baby talk' helps you cover important aspects of early communication.

- 'Baby books' are an exciting way of improving communication skills and laying the basis for later learning.

- 'Baby play' allows you to share ideas for helping parents support their babies' early learning and play.

Baby talk

It is very helpful if you can use the Baby and Me group to help parents 'tune in' to their babies' first attempts at communication. It sometimes comes as a surprise to new parents that babies have their own ways of 'talking' from the earliest stages. Point out how each baby loves to hear their own parent's voice. You can do this very naturally by 'catching the moment' when a baby is responding to the voice and pointing this out to the parent and carer, suggesting that they experiment a bit with quieter or softer tones. Some babies are unsettled and become over-aroused with noise. Point out how clever they are because they have a greater awareness of sound and suggest that they need a quieter voice to pay attention to. Other babies are extra sensitive to sights and might need fewer distractions in order to be at their best. This kind of thinking enables you to help parents tune into their baby's particular strengths and challenges, and tailor their responses to getting the best out of them.

Demonstrate how to place your face close to the baby's, talking and singing gently. From about four months, most babies will love to experiment with different sounds. Model how to talk and then pause, allowing time for the baby to respond with their range of noises – these can sound intriguingly like real words sometimes. By this stage, the rhymes and songs you learned in Chapter 3 will come into their own. By doing so yourselves, take away any of the embarrassment that a new parent might feel about talking with a baby who cannot yet use words back. At all times, respond to the babies as individuals – with all the respect, greetings and farewells that you would give to any adult.

By seven months, babies love to babble. Show parents how to echo the sounds back to the baby and mirror what they are doing. At this stage, baby books are wonderful to share and enjoy together. Some services produce helpful leaflets for families on how to communicate with your 'bump', your baby, your toddler and your pre-school child. We have found these most helpful when we model the suggestions in natural situations as well just giving out the information.

Baby books

'Bookstart' is a project focusing on helping parents to become effective educators of their own babies and young children. It started in Birmingham in 1992 and there are now similar projects all over the UK, including a nationwide BBC campaign 'Babies need books'. Babies at around the nine-month-old stage were each given a book when they were taken along to their local health centres for routine hearing checks. The book came in a bag along with posters and information leaflets for parents explaining the importance of sharing books with their babies and talking about the pictures. It seems that an early start with books provides a reciprocal interaction between parents and baby, a chance to experiment and enjoy time spent together, and the practice needed in order to lead to learning. Many Sure Start schemes are now building on this and have practitioners whose role it is to liaise with library services and promote early book sharing. These practitioners should be well placed to visit any Baby and Me group in order to start the ball rolling for the babies and parents in the group.

Look for picture books with a single bold image on each page rather than embedded in lots of detail. Some groups use digital cameras to take personally meaningful photographs for the baby – Mum, Dad, siblings, the dog, my bottle and so on. These are placed in transparent, plastic wallets and made up into books, the reason being that as the babies get older, tiny fingers find it easier to turn plastic pages than thin paper. Board books are lovely to handle, suck and to begin to turn pages. Books with a tactile element such as something to lift/turn/touch/poke provide added interest for older babies and nowadays there are even books to sniff. Your local library will show you their range of baby books and it is well worthwhile to arrange a group visit or ask for a boxed selection.

Baby play

We arrange for boxes of colourful baby toys to be delivered to our group each session from a toy library and aim for a balance between the novel and the familiar. Without making it too obvious, we 'model' ways of interacting with the baby using the toys and then draw the carer's attention to the wonderful effect the toy is having. Many groups then offer to lend out a toy to bring back next session, using the usual toy library lending system.

Our most popular play material is a set of very bright and colourful chiffon scarves, purchased very cheaply from the local market. These are sucked, waved, cuddled, used to play 'peep bo' and generally enjoyed. It does mean a gentle hand washing of all the scarves after each session, but we have found it well worthwhile.

You might also find it helpful to have some guidelines of the ways in which play and development can be encouraged and enjoyed at each stage.

One set of materials aimed at families with babies and young children is the 'Playsense' pack and this can easily be dipped into and shared during a Baby and Me session. The Playsense materials are a guide and resource for parents and main carers who are interested in watching and developing the play of their babies and young children under three (Barnard and Melidis, 2000). They are produced by the National Association of Toy and Leisure Libraries (see page 42 for their address).

A series of attractive colour-coded cards are organised into four broad areas of play and development: thinking and imaginative play; belonging and connecting; language play; and movement play. Within each area, there are eight stepping stones representing common pathways of learning between birth and around 36 months of age. Each stepping stone card has a section 'have you noticed?', suggesting typical behaviour and ways of playing which parents might notice around each stage, though it is pointed out that each child has their own unique way of learning and growing. There are also suggestions for building on and encouraging play at around that stage. This approach fits well with any toy library that you might have access to, since parents are encouraged to use and borrow toys and playthings at various stages to support them as they support their babies' development through play.

Some groups develop handouts to support the work they are doing with baby play. There is an example of the kind of information that parents find interesting to share on the next page. This section is adapted from *100 Number Games for ages 0 to 3* (Mortimer, 2003) and is part of a series on games that parents can do with their babies and young children to support early learning and fun.

Did you know how clever your baby is?

Your new baby is learning how to make sense of the world. There are sounds, shapes, movements, colours and feelings all around. At first these are a buzzing confusion of sensations and your baby does not yet have any sense of how they are linked together, or even that he or she is a little person in his or her own right. Yet your baby has been born almost pre-programmed to learn and will actively be seeking out sounds, sights and touch as the weeks go by.

- Your baby begins to learn that the sound of the door in the morning means that you are coming into the room and he or she turns to look.

- Your baby begins to learn that the fist waving in front of his or her eyes belongs to him or her and it can be moved at will.

- Your baby begins to learn that he or she can knock a play centre and it makes a sound that can be repeated.

- Your baby also begins to learn that if a toy disappears momentarily from view, it still exists to be found again.

This ability to learn that toys and people continue to exist even when your baby cannot see them is called 'object permanence' and is a vital early stage to understanding about the world. This is clever baby work! This is why 'peep bo' and hiding games are so important and enjoyable to your baby.

You can start to encourage your baby to learn from a very early age. Young children learn best through playing and through interactions and games with people and objects around them. Play that is best for development is play that is at just the right developmental level for the child, or that which slightly stretches him or her. If you can provide the right opportunities, the right materials and be supportive and encouraging, you will help your child become a successful learner.

Chapter 6

Evaluation

This chapter contains suggestions for evaluation and reporting back to management committees.

Asking for feedback

You might ask the parents or carers directly about what they thought about Baby and Me once their sessions are over. Here is a form that you can adapt, using it either as a written questionnaire or a semi-structured interview.

Baby and Me Evaluation **Confidential** Thank you for attending the group. We hope you found it useful and enjoyable. Please give us some anonymous feedback to help us plan future groups – do feel free to be open with us.
Before the group began Did you find the home visit helpful?   Yes   No Why? - Was the information given to you: Too much?   Just right?   Too little? - Did you feel prepared for the first session?   Yes   No
Coming to the group Did you enjoy coming?   Yes   No Why?

What difference has the group made:

to you?

to your baby?

- -

What changes in the group do you feel are needed?

- -

What activity did you find most useful? (Please number 1 as most useful and 4 as least)

    Music
    Talking to other parents
    Talking to the professionals
    Other – please tell us what

- -

Was the venue suitable?   Yes   No

- -

Would you recommend the group to
other families?   Yes   No

Why?

- -

Thank you for your time.
From the Baby and Me Team

Reporting to management

It is helpful if you can report back to management regularly on the perceived effectiveness of these groups. One reason for this is that it is an intervention involving high staffing levels and, unless you can show that the group actually changes patterns of parenting, it might not be seen as 'value for money'. We have, therefore, found it helpful to report not only on parents' evaluations, but our own evaluations on how we feel those families will now cope and whether we have been able to work preventatively by reducing later problems and referrals for specialist help. This sometimes involved using wider service statistics, including patterns of referral to social services. Here are some examples of simple evaluation studies.

The future

Our own plans for the future involve placing Baby and Me firmly within a whole scaffold of support for Sure Start families. We feel that they should be more parent-led and arise from clearly expressed family needs rather than what we decide is needed for them. We have seen enough benefits from the families and children involved to recommend the groups for other areas.

Snapshot of practice

It is only the second session of this Baby and Me group held in a local Sure Start office in a converted school. The room is large, airy and carpeted and curtained prettily. There is new furniture with comfortable chairs arranged in a circle. On a side table away from the babies there are flasks, mugs and hot drink-making equipment. As I enter the room, the atmosphere is calm and relaxed. None of the babies is unsettled. Around the circle sit five mothers and their babies, one father and a couple of extra friends. The youngest baby is four weeks old and the oldest about eight months. Some sit up on knees and are engaged in 'gumming' colourful scarves or exploring colourful and mouthable rattles. One is asleep in a cradle and another is breastfeeding. Spaced around the circle are two Sure Start professionals and a health visitor. There is an easy chatter

---

going on. In the centre of the circle is a play mat with very colourful activity centres for the babies to lie under and knock. There are plastic mirrors, rattles and baby toys. There are also spare bouncing cradles that are being positioned so that mothers can smile at and sing to their babies. A new mother arrives; it is her first visit. She is welcomed by one of the professionals who draws a chair up next to her and admires the new baby. She uses this moment to catch up on how mother and baby are doing and to give time for the two to settle in. After a few minutes, she personally introduces the new arrivals to the others in the circle.

The music leader reaches for a guitar and starts to sing quietly 'If you're happy and you know it'. The mothers gather babies onto their knees and start to rock and move them gently. Several people join in with the singing. A second professional then takes centre stage and moves around each baby as the group sing 'We'll rock hello to Dominic' (etc.). The singing and actions flow smoothly for a further 20 minutes, varying from lively to gentle and with everyone either joining in or looking relaxed. At the end, there is a final 'goodbye' song.

There is a little bit of feedback peppering the songs such as 'this one is excellent for changing time'; 'this one makes a good lullaby'; 'look at his face when you do that!', though the information is delivered naturally rather than by way of 'teaching'.

At the end, all members of the group are chatting together easily. They talk about recent newspaper headlines that singing to babies is good for them. They share information and one or two have words with the health visitor for advice and support. Some of the mothers come to hear of other Sure Start groups being run in their locality and make arrangements to attend with their friends. There are 'see you next week's as they leave. The professionals decide that they are meeting an unmet need and vow to continue.

References

Barnard, C. and Melidis, S. (2000) *Playsense: A Guide and Resource for Play for Babies and Young Children.* London: National Association of Toy and Leisure Libraries.

Mortimer, H. (2003) *100 Number Games for ages 0 to 3.* Leamington Spa: Scholastic.

Mortimer, H. (2005) *RUMPUS: Planning behaviour groups for parents and carers of young children.* Lichfield: QEd Publications.

Mortimer, H. (2005) *Music Makers: Music circle times to include everyone.* Lichfield: QEd Publications.

Useful books

Diamond, E. (2002) *An Early Start in Music.* International Music Publications.

Harrop, B., Friend, L. and Gadsby, D. (1975) *Okki-tokki-unga: Action Songs for Children.* London: A & C Black.

Kleiner, L. (1998) *Kids Make Music, Babies Make Music Too!* Miami: Warner Brothers Publications.

Matterson, E. (Ed.) (2004) *This Little Puffin.* London: Puffin Books.

Pavelko, V. and Scott, L.B. (1976) *Apusskidu: Songs for Children.* London: A & C Black.

Powell, H. (1983) *Game-Songs with Prof. Dogg's Troupe.* London: A & C Black.

Quinn, M. and T. (1995) *From Pram to Primary: Parenting small children from birth to age six or seven.* Newry: Family Caring Trust.

Roberts, S. (2004) *Lively Time Playsongs: Baby's Active Day in Songs and Pictures.* London: A & C Black.

Roberts, S. (2004) *Sleepy Time Playsongs: Baby's Restful Day in Songs and Pictures.* London: A & C Black.

Useful resources

Early Learning Centre for tapes, instruments and song books.
Tel: 08705 352352
Website: www.elc.co.uk

LDA, Duke Street, Wisbech, Cambridgeshire PE13 2AE
Tel: 0845 120 4776
Website: www.ldalearning.com

Music Education Supplies Ltd, 101 Banstead Road South, Sutton,
Surrey SM2 5LH

NESArnold for musical instruments and props.
Tel: 0845 120 4525
Website: www.nesarnold.co.uk

Step by Step (SBS) for colourful and more unusual musical instruments
suitable for early years and SEN.
SBS, Lee Fold, Hyde, Cheshire SK14 4LL
Tel: 0845 3001089
Website: www.sbs-educational.co.uk

Useful organisations

Barnardo's, Tanners Lane, Barkingside, Ilford, Essex IG6 1QG
Tel: 020 8550 8822   Fax: 020 8551 6870
Website: www.barnardos.org.uk
Provides care and support for children in need and their families, with
projects throughout the UK. A catalogue can be obtained from Barnardo's
Child Care Publications, Barnardo's Trading Estate, Paycocke Road,
Basildon, Essex SS14 3DR.

National Children's Bureau, 8 Wakley Street, London EC1V 7QE
Tel: 020 7843 6000 or 020 7843 6008 (library enquiry line: 10am–12 noon,
and 2pm–4pm)
Fax: 020 7843 6007
Email: library@ncb.org.uk
Website: www.ncb.org.uk

A multidisciplinary organisation concerned with the promotion and identification of the interests of all children and young people. It is also involved in research, policy and practice development, and consultancy.

National NEWPIN, Sutherland House, 35 Sutherland Square,
London SE17 3EE
Tel: 020 7703 6326
Fax: 020 7701 2660
Email: newpin@nationalnewpin.freeserve.co.uk
Website: www.newpin.org.uk
Offers parents and children an opportunity to achieve positive changes in their lives and relationships, and break the cycle of destructive family behaviour. There are several centres, mainly in the London area. Newpin offers parenting skills training programmes and includes a fathers' project.

The National Association of Toy and Leisure Libraries, 68 Churchway,
London NW1 1LT
Tel: 020 7255 4600
Email: admin@playmatters.co.uk
Website: www.natll.org.uk

PIPPIN Parents in Partnership – Parent Infant Network, Derwood,
Todds Green, Stevenage, Herts SG1 2JE
Tel: 01438 748487
Fax: 01438 748182
Website: www.pippin.org.uk
This national charity, which promotes positive early family and parent-infant relationships, aims to maintain and improve the emotional health of families during the period surrounding the birth of a new baby. It offers parentcraft classes, and a range of projects which include work with fathers.